SOLDIER JUMPING CONTEST

BIBLE INFOGRAPHICS
FOR Kids

HARVEST HOUSE PUBLISHERS
Eugene, Oregon

CREATED BY HARVEST HOUSE **BIBLE** INFOGRAPHICS **TEAM**

Illustrations by
BRIAN HURST

HEATHER GREEN **KYLE HATFIELD** **NICOLE DOUGHERTY** **KYLER DOUGHERTY**

BOOK COVER DESIGN

 **SPECIAL THANKS** ➤ **JEFF MARION**   **GENE SKINNER**   **DEREK DOUGHERTY**   **BRYCE WILLIAMSON**

Library of Congress Cataloging-in-Publication Data

Names: Harvest House Publishers.

Title: Bible infographics for kids.

Description: Eugene, Oregon : Harvest House Publishers, 2018. | Includes bibliographical references.

Identifiers: LCCN 2017028151 (print) | LCCN 2017034594 (ebook) | ISBN 9780736972437 (ebook) | ISBN 9780736972420 (hardcover)

Subjects: LCSH: Bible—Criticism, interpretation, etc.—Juvenile literature. | Bible—Miscellanea.

Classification: LCC BS539 (ebook) | LCC BS539 .B53 2018 (print) | DDC 220.6/1—dc23

LC record available at https://lccn.loc.gov/2017028151

Bible Infographics for Kids
Copyright © 2018 by Harvest House Publishers
Published by Harvest House Publishers
Eugene, Oregon 97408
www.harvesthousepublishers.com
ISBN 978-0-7369-7242-0 (hardcover)

Printed in China
18 19 20 21 22 23 24 25 26 / RDS / 10 9 8 7 6 5 4 3 2

A Picture Is Worth a Thousand Words

Have you ever heard this saying before?
It means that seeing something can be far more powerful than just reading about it.

Wow! Look at this craze-mazing rainbow!

Someone could describe a rainbow...

A Rainbow is a naturally occurring phenomenon. A refraction of light in water particles creates seven colors (red, orange, yellow, green, blue, indigo, and violet—ROYGBIV). A rainbow usually appears as a single arch but sometimes as a double or even triple arch...

Can you imagine it now?

...ZZZ

....but it won't be the same as if you saw it yourself.

That's what an infographic does. It helps you see information that might otherwise be hard to understand. The infographics in this book will help you learn a lot of fun facts and incredible information about God's Word.

FROM THE **SERIOUS** TO THE **SILLY** YOU'LL SCORE **EPIC BIBLE KNOWLEDGE**

Are you ready to begin your
OUT-OF-THIS-WORLD infographic adventure?

LET'S GO!

CONTENTS

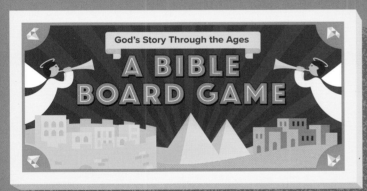

THE BIBLE GOD'S EPICALLY AWESOME BOOK

THE 66 BOOKS OF THE BIBLE

Old Testament—39 books

- **The Law** (5) Genesis–Deuteronomy
- **History** (12) Joshua–Esther
- **Wisdom & Poetry** (5) Job–Song of Solomon
- **Prophets** (17) Isaiah–Malachi

New Testament—27 books

- **The Gospels** (4) Matthew–John
- **Church History** (1) Acts
- **Epistles (Letters)** (21) Romans–Jude
- **Apocalypse** (1) Revelation

There are **31,102** verses in the Bible.

Old Testament **23,145** verses | New Testament **7,957** verses

THE BIBLE WAS WRITTEN...

...by more than **40 authors**

Samuel, a priest

David, a king

Joshua, a general

Nehemiah, a cupbearer

Daniel, a prime minister

Luke, a physician

Peter, a fisherman

Matthew, a tax collector

Paul, a rabbi, Pharisee, and tentmaker

A cupbearer tasted the king's drinks to make sure they weren't poisoned.

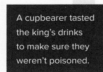

...in many **different places**

Moses, in the wilderness

Daniel, in a foreign emperor's palace

Paul, in prison and traveling the world

Luke, traveling with Paul

John, in exile on the island of Patmos

On three different continents— Asia, Africa, and Europe

...in **3 different languages**

Hebrew (almost all of the Old Testament) Hebrew was written and read from right to left and without any vowels.

 **?sys cntns sht knht y d thW**

Aramaic (parts of the Old and New Testaments) The Israelites began to speak Aramaic when they were captive in Assyria and Babylon.

Koine Greek (most of New Testament) This was the common "street language" people used throughout the Roman Empire, different from classical Greek, which Aristotle, Socrates, Plato, and Homer used.

...over a span of about **1500 years** (it was worth the wait!)

THENEWTESTAMENTWASORIGINALLYW RITTENLIKETHISWITHNOSPACESBETWE ENWORDSITHADNOPUNCTUATIONAND NOPARAGRAPHBREAKSITWASWRITTEN WITHNOVERSENUMBERSCHAPTERNUM BERSORSECTIONHEADINGSTHESEWERE ADDEDLATERTOHELPREADERSLIKEYOU

OF ALL TIME
BESTSELLING
BOOK
EVERY YEAR

5 Billion

4 Billion

3 Billion

THE
BIBLE

2 Billion

1 Billion

■ **The Hunger Games series**
by Suzanne Collins
23 million

■ **The Lord of the Rings series**
by J.R.R. Tolkien
150 million

■ **Harry Potter series**
by J.K. Rowling
500 million

■ *Don Quixote*
by Miguel de Cervantes
500 million

ALL THE BIBLES SOLD WOULD...

REACH THE MOON
almost
3 TIMES

CIRCLE THE EARTH
more than
28½ TIMES

The King James Bible
has more than
780,000 WORDS
(or **3,116,000** characters).

Typing the entire Bible
would take more than
260 HOURS.

That would take almost
11 DAYS STRAIGHT.

No sleep for you!

The Bible has been translated into many more languages than any other book.

The Entire Bible:

636 🙂
(even Klingon and Emoji)

A Portion of the Bible:

3,223

In Progress:

2,422
in **165** countries

HOW ON EARTH

DAY 1

GOD SEPARATED **LIGHT** & **DARK**.

WITH NO **MOON**, NO **SUN**, AND NO **STARS**...

God was the light!

"I am the light of the world. Whoever follows me will never walk in darkness, but will have the light of life." John 8:12

DAY 2

HE SEPARATED **EARTH** & **SKY**.

THE EARTH IS **MOVING FAST!**
Standing on the equator, you'd be spinning at

1,000 MPH

and zooming around the sun at

67,000 MPH!

! **Why don't we get dizzy?** Because everything around us is moving at the same speed, we feel as if we aren't moving at all.

DAY 3

HE GATHERED THE **LAND** & **SEA** AND PRODUCED **VEGETATION**.

THE **EARTH'S SURFACE** IS **28%** LAND & **72%** SEA

! The oceans are **less than 1% of the earth's volume**. More than 866 of them could fit inside the earth!

DAY 7

HE **RESTED** ON THE SEVENTH DAY.
God commanded the Israelites to rest and worship. They did this on Saturday and called it the Sabbath.

Remember the Sabbath day by keeping it holy. Exodus 20:8

DID IT ALL BEGIN?

DAY 4

HE MADE THE **SUN & MOON** AND **STARS & PLANETS**.

GOD MADE **TWO GREAT LIGHTS**

THE GREATER LIGHT TO GOVERN THE **DAY**	THE LESSER LIGHT TO GOVERN THE **NIGHT**

Genesis 1:16

The **SUN** is **400x LARGER** than the **MOON**.	The **MOON** is **400x CLOSER** than the **SUN**.

! That's why they appear to be the **same size in the sky**.

DAY 5

HE CREATED THE **CREATURES** OF THE **SEA & SKY**.

EGG **HATCHING TIME**

14 days Canaries

21 days Chickens

28 days Ducks

35 days Swans

42 days Ostriches

! Many eggs hatch in **multiples of 7 days**.

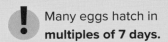

DAY 6

HE MADE **ANIMALS** ON LAND AND **MAN & WOMAN** IN HIS IMAGE.

God formed a **MAN ("ADAM")** אָדָם
Out of the dust of the **GROUND ("ADAMA")** אֲדָמָה

God then caused Adam to fall into a deep sleep and **formed Eve, the first woman,** out of Adam's rib.

! **Did you know** that the elements that make up the human body can be found in the earth's soil?

God made everything—from the tiniest bug to the biggest galaxy—and it was very good.

Genesis 1–2

NOAH'S ARK
HOW BIG WAS IT?

The Bible measures the ark in cubits.

HOW BIG IS A CUBIT?

1 CUBIT

18 INCHES

The water from the flood covered the tallest mountain peak by

22 FEET!

The water would have stood over

29,050'

above sea level! That's a depth of

5.5 MILES

555'
Washington Monument

450'
Noah's Ark

360'
Football Field

232'
Boeing 747

211'   **160'**   **75'   55'**

GENESIS 6–8

The ark was big enough to hold

55,000
SPECIES OF ANIMALS

NOAH'S ARK		WHITE HOUSE
100,000 SQUARE FEET	VS	**55,000** SQUARE FEET

That's the same volume as

7,453,506
SOCCER BALLS.

If you laid each soccer ball next to each other, they would stretch

1,030 MILES!

That's like driving from

LOUISVILLE, KY, TO **AUSTIN, TX.**

For the same square footage, that's

71,620 PIZZAS,

which would be a pizza a day for over

196 YEARS.

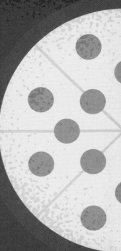

GOD BUILDS HIS NATION

The Story of Abraham, His Descendants, and the Birth of Israel

God made a promise to Abraham when he was **70 years old**: *He took him outside and said, **"Look up at the sky and count the stars—if indeed you can count them." Then he said to him, "So shall your offspring be."***

Genesis 15:5

MOST MENTIONED MAN #7 IN THE BIBLE

ABRAHAM

He was **100 YEARS OLD** when Isaac was born.

OBEYING GOD, he was ready to sacrifice his son Isaac, but the Lord sent an angel to stop him.

LIVED TO BE 175

MOST MENTIONED WOMAN #1 IN THE BIBLE

SARAH

STRUGGLED WITH WAITING on God to fulfill His promises but was still chosen to be the mother of nations.

She was **90 YEARS OLD** when Isaac was born. His birth was a gift from God.

HA HA HA HA HA

MOST MENTIONED WOMAN #4 IN THE BIBLE

REBEKAH

Gave birth to Jacob and Esau, **THE FIRST TWINS** mentioned in the Bible.

MOST MENTIONED MAN #15 IN THE BIBLE

ISAAC

His name means **"HE LAUGHS"** because of his parents' reaction to God when He told them they would have a son at ages 90 and 100.

MOST MENTIONED MAN #4 IN THE BIBLE

JACOB

Jacob and his mother **TRICKED ISAAC** into giving him the blessing of the firstborn, which belonged to Esau.

Was **RENAMED "ISRAEL"** by God.

Jacob's 12 sons became known as...

THE 12 TRIBES OF ISRAEL

| REUBEN | SIMEON | LEVI | JUDAH | DAN | NAPHTALI | GAD | ASHER | ISSACHAR | ZEBULUN | BENJAMIN |

Instead of inheriting land of their own, Levi's descendants become the priests who dwell in all tribes.

DANIEL

SAMSON

It was foretold that the Messiah would dwell in their land. Galilee, where Jesus lived, is in Naphtali!

KING SAUL

JESUS

BARNABAS

JOHN THE BAPTIST

MORDECAI

MOSES

APOSTLE PAUL

Keep reading to see what role Moses plays in the story of God's nation...

MOSES

MOST MENTIONED MAN #3 IN THE BIBLE

Four generations later, he led the Israelites (the name given to the descendants of Abraham) out of slavery in Egypt. It was called **THE EXODUS** (see more on page 14) and brought them one step closer to the Promised Land, where God's promise to Abraham was completed.

600,000 MEN (over the age of 20) **+ WOMEN + CHILDREN** (and all their flocks and herds) **= approximately 3-4 MILLION PEOPLE**

Roughly the population of Los Angeles.

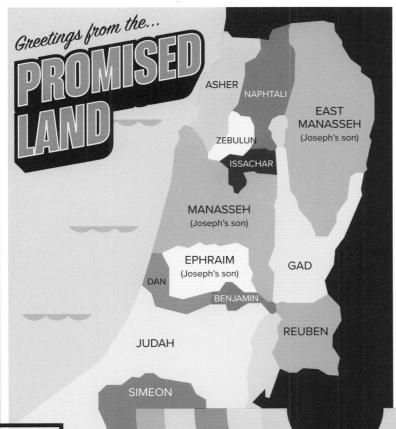

Greetings from the...
PROMISED LAND

ASHER
NAPHTALI
EAST MANASSEH (Joseph's son)
ZEBULUN
ISSACHAR
MANASSEH (Joseph's son)
EPHRAIM (Joseph's son)
DAN
GAD
BENJAMIN
REUBEN
JUDAH
SIMEON

! DID YOU KNOW:
THE NAKED EYE CAN SEE **4,548 STARS** IN THE NIGHT SKY, AND THERE ARE BETWEEN **100** BILLION and **400** BILLION **STARS IN OUR GALAXY** (THE MILKY WAY).

MOST MENTIONED MAN #9 IN THE BIBLE

JOSEPH
— EPHRAIM — MANASSEH
— JOSHUA
— SAMUEL

Jacob gave Joseph the blessing usually for the firstborn. Joseph received two portions of land in the name of his sons, Ephraim and Manasseh.

JOSEPH'S ROBE OF MANY COLORS

SYMBOLIZED his status as favorite son, the blessing of his birth, and his gift of prophetic dreams.

FORESHADOWED his future blessings.

INTENSIFIED his brothers' jealousy.

TRICKED Jacob into believing he was dead.

THE 10 PLAGUES

GOD'S RIGHTEOUS DISPLAY OF POWER

When Pharaoh wouldn't release the Israelites from captivity,
God brought ten plagues upon Egypt, each worse than the one before.

Plague (*noun*) : a widespread disaster

1 WATER INTO BLOOD
Exodus 7:14-25

The Egyptians worshipped the Nile River—until it instantly turned to blood! All the fish died, the river stank, and the water became undrinkable.

2 FROGS
Exodus 8:1-14

One or two frogs are cute, but God caused them to come up onto the ground by the thousands. They were everywhere! Just imagine the noise.

A group of frogs is called an "army." God's army of frogs covered all of Egypt.

CROAK!

XING

3 GNATS (or Fleas or Lice)
Exodus 8:16-19

Egyptians were very concerned with cleanliness, so they shaved off all their body hair and wore wigs. One reason they did this was to prevent lice. You can only imagine how terrible this plague would have felt.

4 FLIES
Exodus 8:20-32

Imagine swarms of flies covering Egypt! In 2014, near the Mississippi River, swarms of flies were so large and thick, they caused numerous car accidents.

5 DEAD LIVESTOCK
Exodus 9:1-7

Holy cow! Egyptians used cattle for food, milk, and leather. Some of their false gods even looked like cattle.

6 BOILS
Exodus 9:8-12

The people and animals of Egypt broke out in painful boils—terrible sores on their skin. Pharaoh's magicians were unable to stand because of the extreme pain.

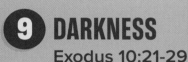

OUCH!

7 HAIL
Exodus 9:13-33

Heads up! This was the worst storm Egypt ever experienced—animals, people, and crops were all struck down.

LARGEST RECORDED HAILSTONE

18.62"   7.9"

1.94 pounds

8 LOCUSTS
Exodus 10:1-18

God sent a swarm of locusts to devour what little was left after the hailstorm.

A locust is the same size as a paper clip.

The largest recorded **SWARM OF LOCUSTS** covered **198,000 MILES** an area greater than **the SIZE OF CALIFORNIA!**

9 DARKNESS
Exodus 10:21-29

Who turned out the lights? God did. For three entire days, the Egyptians were in total darkness. They couldn't see each other or move around. Meanwhile, God's people had all the light they needed.

10 DEATH OF THE FIRSTBORN
Exodus 11–12

In the final plague, God struck down firstborn sons—including Pharaoh's own son. The families with blood on their doorposts were **passed over.**

GOD'S DISPLAY OF POWER HAD A PURPOSE

Each plague God sent was aimed at one of the false gods of Egypt. He was demonstrating His authority as the one true God.

Soon after the last plague, God delivered His people out of Egypt and one step closer to the land He promised Abraham.

> "I will bring judgment on all the gods of Egypt. I am the LORD."
> Exodus 12:12

GOD LAYS DOWN THE LAW

DON'T DO THIS

365
NEGATIVE COMMANDS

The same as the number of days in a year.

THE LAW CONTAINS
613
COMMANDS

DO THIS

248
POSITIVE COMMANDS

The same as the number of bones and organs in the human body.

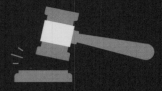

DO 613 LAWS SEEM LIKE A LOT TO FOLLOW?
Consider that United States federal law includes more than **300,000** rules and regulations, and more laws are created every year!

THE MORAL LAW
HOW TO KNOW RIGHT FROM WRONG

Exodus 20:1-17

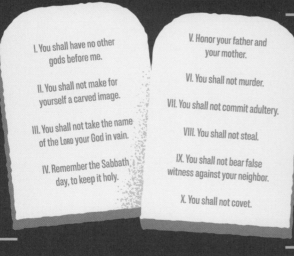

I. You shall have no other gods before me.

II. You shall not make for yourself a carved image.

III. You shall not take the name of the Lord your God in vain.

IV. Remember the Sabbath day, to keep it holy.

V. Honor your father and your mother.

VI. You shall not murder.

VII. You shall not commit adultery.

VIII. You shall not steal.

IX. You shall not bear false witness against your neighbor.

X. You shall not covet.

LOVE GOD

LOVE YOUR NEIGHBOR

THE TEN COMMANDMENTS were given to Moses on stone tablets and kept inside the Ark of the Covenant.

WHAT IS THE GREATEST COMMANDMENT IN THE LAW?

Jesus said it was: "'**LOVE THE LORD YOUR GOD** with all your heart and with all your soul and with all your mind.' This is the first and greatest commandment. And the second is like it: '**LOVE YOUR NEIGHBOR** as yourself.' All the Law and the Prophets hang on these two commandments."
Matthew 22:36-40

THE SOCIAL LAW
HOW THE NATION OF ISRAEL WAS TO LIVE

Exodus 21:1–23:17

TREATMENT OF SERVANTS
After 6 full years of service, they were set free.

STOLEN PROPERTY
If your ox, donkey, or sheep was stolen, it should be restored and another one given to you—two for the price of one!

PROTECTION FOR WIDOWS & ORPHANS
God showed His compassion for the most vulnerable members of Israel by establishing harsh penalties for crimes against widows or orphans.

NATIONAL HOLIDAYS
God established several festivals for Israel to celebrate, including these three:

- **Feast of Unleavened Bread**— celebrating Israel's deliverance from slavery in Egypt

- **Feast of Harvest (or Firstfruits)**— celebrating the beginning of the wheat harvest

- **Feast of Ingathering (or Pentecost)**— celebrating the end of the wheat harvest

THE CEREMONIAL LAW
HOW ISRAEL WAS TO INTERACT WITH GOD

Exodus 25–30

GOD'S HEALTH CODE

God established rules to keep His people healthy and the population growing.
Some of these guidelines were way ahead of their time and still make sense today.

FIGHTING GERMS
Leviticus 17:15

God stated the Israelites needed to use running water to wash away germs. In 1845, a doctor discovered the death rate for mothers giving birth went down from 30% to 2% when doctors washed their hands in running water rather than in a shared basin.

EATING A HEALTHY DIET
Leviticus 11

God stated that the Israelites shouldn't eat pigs, camels, sea creatures without fins or scales, birds of prey, flying insects with four legs, weasels, lizards, rats, and bats. Was He just being picky? No. We now know these animals are likely to carry disease.

MEDICAL QUARANTINE
Leviticus 13:45-46

Long before the field of medicine began quarantining contagious patients, God told the Israelites to isolate people with infectious diseases until they were cured.

SOIL CONSERVATION
Leviticus 23:22; 25:4-5

God instructed farmers to leave the gleanings during harvest, not to harvest the sides of their fields, and to let their land "rest" (to grow nothing on it) every seven years. Today, we know these instructions served a few important purposes:

1) Gleanings provided food for the poor.
2) The leftover row along the sides limited wind erosion.
3) Soil minerals were maintained.

> **gleaning** (*noun*) :
> leftover grain (or other produce) from a harvest

ANIMAL SACRIFICE
Exodus 29:36

The law required **atonement for sin** through animal sacrifice. Only through a **blood sacrifice** could the Jewish people atone for their sinful actions.

> **atone** (*verb*) :
> to reconcile or make amends

> **sacrifice** (*verb*) :
> to offer up something precious for a cause or reason

JESUS BECAME THE ULTIMATE BLOOD SACRIFICE FOR ALL OUR SINS

Jesus's last words before His death were **"It is finished"** (John 19:30). This means when Jesus died on the cross, He paid the full penalty for our sins—past, present, and future. **That's why there is no longer a need for animal sacrifice.**

God made him who had no sin to be sin for us, so that in him we might become the righteousness of God.
2 Corinthians 5:21

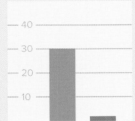

WHAT'S THE DEAL WITH

God Dwelling with His People

God has **always** desired to dwell with His people.

After Adam and Eve sinned, they were **banished from the garden and from God's presence.** Adam and Eve represent all of us. Genesis 3:23

Through Jesus's **permanent sacrifice, we can be in God's presence** without making animal sacrifices or going to a physical building.

"Look! God's dwelling place is now among the people, **and he will dwell with them.** They will be his people, and God himself will be with them and be their God."
Revelation 21:3

GOD WITH HUMANITY

SIN

GOD'S PRESENCE ONLY THROUGH ANIMAL SACRIFICE

JESUS

GOD WITH HUMANITY FOREVER

THE GARDEN OF EDEN Genesis 2–3

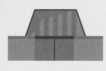

God Himself walked with Adam and Eve in the garden.

 Large amounts of gold and precious stones are mentioned.

 God used animal skins to cover Adam and Eve's nakedness.

 God placed cherubim (angels) and a flaming sword on the east side of the garden to guard the way to the tree of life.

THE TABERNACLE Exodus 25, 29, 37

God commanded the Israelites to build a **temporary and portable** dwelling so He could be with them.

 Gold and precious stones adorned the tabernacle.

 The priests had to offer animal sacrifices to be in God's presence.

 Cherubim statues were placed on the Ark of the Covenant where God's presence would appear.

THE TEMPLE 1 Kings 6:11-13

God commanded King Solomon to build a **permanent and elaborate** building where God could be with His people.

 Gold and precious stones adorned the temple.

 As in the tabernacle, only through animal sacrifices could the priests enter God's presence.

Cherubim statues were placed in the Most Holy Place.

JESUS John 1:14

Jesus was like a tabernacle—**in Him, God dwelled with us.**

In Jesus, God walked with us, just as He walked with Adam and Eve in the Garden of Eden.

 Jesus is the most precious stone of all—the cornerstone of our faith. 1 Peter 2:4-6

 Jesus is the Lamb of God whose death covered our sin. Revelation 5:8-9

 Angels announced Jesus's birth and resurrection.

THE CHURCH Ephesians 2:21-22

The church is now God's temple because **the Holy Spirit dwells in us.**

THE NEW JERUSALEM Revelation 21

When Jesus returns, He will create a new earth and a new Jerusalem, **where we can live with Him.**

 The streets are paved with gold, and the gates and foundations made with precious stones.

 Angels are present in the throne room of heaven and will announce Jesus's return.

THE TABERNACLE?

God Dwelling with Israel

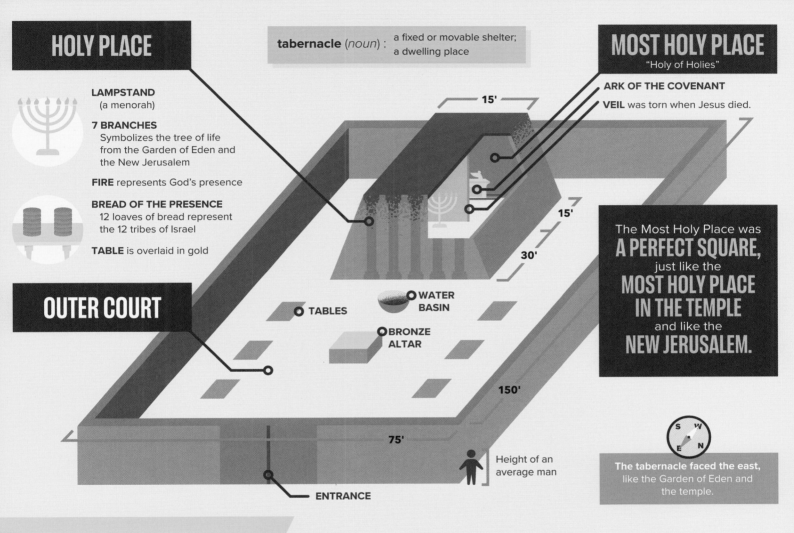

tabernacle (*noun*) : a fixed or movable shelter; a dwelling place

HOLY PLACE

LAMPSTAND
(a menorah)

7 BRANCHES
Symbolizes the tree of life from the Garden of Eden and the New Jerusalem

FIRE represents God's presence

BREAD OF THE PRESENCE
12 loaves of bread represent the 12 tribes of Israel

TABLE is overlaid in gold

OUTER COURT

TABLES

WATER BASIN

BRONZE ALTAR

15'

15'

30'

150'

75'

ENTRANCE

Height of an average man

MOST HOLY PLACE
"Holy of Holies"

ARK OF THE COVENANT

VEIL was torn when Jesus died.

The Most Holy Place was
A PERFECT SQUARE,
just like the
MOST HOLY PLACE IN THE TEMPLE
and like the
NEW JERUSALEM.

The tabernacle faced the east, like the Garden of Eden and the temple.

ARK OF THE COVENANT

ATONEMENT COVER (or mercy seat)
A gold cover for the Ark with cherubim at the ends. Drops of blood from the sacrifices were sprinkled on it. Where God's presence appeared.

WOOD OVERLAID WITH GOLD

POLES FOR CARRYING
It was portable—God was not confined to one spot, but moved with the Israelites wherever they went.

INSIDE THE ARK

THE TEN COMMANDMENTS
The basis of the covenant between God and Israel

A POT OF MANNA
A reminder of God's faithfulness to care for His people

AARON'S BUDDING STAFF
A sign that Aaron was God's chosen high priest

19

ODD AND AMAZING

Tall but True Tales from the Bible

FISHY MONEY
Matthew 17:27

Jesus tells Peter to go fishing. In the mouth of the **FIRST FISH HE CATCHES,** he'll find a coin to pay a tax.

A DONKEY SPEAKS ITS MIND
Numbers 22:21-30

When Balaam disobeys God, God blocks his way with an angel that only Balaam's donkey can see. Balaam beats the donkey—until **GOD MAKES THE DONKEY TALK!** Finally Balaam sees the angel—and the error of his ways.

HEY!

ELISHA'S BALD REVENGE
2 Kings 2:23-25

Some young guys make fun of Elisha's bald head. Elisha **CURSES THEM IN THE NAME OF THE LORD,** and suddenly two bears come out of the woods and maul 42 of them.

RIGHT ON THE NOSE

In 2002, a man caught a swordfish, put his wedding ring on its nose, and released it. Incredibly, **THREE YEARS LATER,** he caught the same swordfish—and it still had the ring on its nose!

LOTS O' DONKEYS

Donkeys appear **142 TIMES** in the Bible.*
*in the NIV

A **DONKEY'S JAW** was used to kill 1,000 men.
Judges 15:15-16

Joseph and Mary likely **RODE A DONKEY** to Bethlehem.
Luke 2:4-5

JESUS RODE into Jerusalem on a donkey.
Matthew 21:1-11

WHO ARE YOU CALLING BALD?

These "young guys" could have been as old as 30—they knew what they were doing. Besides, there would have been at least 42 of them ganging up on Elisha. That's not cool, but **GOD HAD ELISHA'S BACK.**

VS

20

BIBLE STORIES

Sometimes truth is stranger than fiction—even in the Bible.

JESUS CURSES THE FIG TREE
Matthew 21:18-19; Mark 11:12-13

Jesus curses a fig tree that has leaves but no figs, and the fig tree *immediately* withers. Trees usually take **WEEKS OR EVEN MONTHS** to wither.

JACOB WRESTLES WITH GOD
Genesis 32:22-32

Jacob wrestles with a mysterious man all night, but finally the man touches Jacob's hip, injuring him. Jacob promises to let the man go if the man gives him a blessing. The man agrees, and Jacob is blessed. Jacob also receives a new name—Israel—because **HE STRUGGLED WITH GOD AND OVERCAME.**

JACOB VS GOD
ROUND 1

ELISHA'S MAGIC BONES?
2 Kings 13:21

Sometime after Elisha died, a group of Israelites were burying a man. When they saw a band of raiders, they panicked and threw the man's body into Elisha's tomb. When the body touched Elisha's bones, **THE MAN CAME TO LIFE.** God performed a miracle!

THAT'LL TEACH YOU, FIG TREE

Like the fig tree, the religious people of Jesus's day appeared to be alive but weren't producing any **SPIRITUAL FRUIT**—love, joy, peace, patience, kindness, goodness, faithfulness, gentleness, and self-control.

THERE'S NO MATCH FOR GOD

THE GUINNESS WORLD RECORD
12 HOURS
2010
LONGEST PRO WRESTLING MATCH

BONES IN THE BIBLE

There are **45 VERSES** about bones in the Bible.

Ezekiel has a **VISION** in which bones come to life as an army.
Ezekiel 37

Jesus **FULFILLED THE PROPHECY** that none of His bones would be broken.
John 19:31-36

MEET THE BIBLE'S MOST
UNIQUE CHARACTERS

DEBORAH
ONLY FEMALE JUDGE

She helped **defeat the great general Sisera** with the aid of Jael, some milk, and a tent peg. She was also a prophet and insisted God's will be done, not hers.

Judges 4

METHUSELAH
OLDEST PERSON

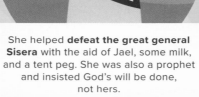

Noah's grandfather **lived 969 years.** The modern record is held by Jeanne Louise Calment, who lived 122 years, 164 days.

Genesis 5:27

ESAU
HAIRIEST BABY

Esau was the son of Isaac and Rebekah and the twin brother of Jacob. At birth, he was so hairy, he **looked like he was wearing a coat.**

Genesis 25:25

LOT'S WIFE
ONLY PERSON TURNED INTO A PILLAR OF SALT

When the Lord rained down burning sulfur on Sodom and Gomorrah, **Lot's wife hung around a little too long.**

Genesis 19:26

MAHER-SHALAL-HASH-BAZ
LONGEST NAME

Hello My Name Is
Maher-Shalal-Hash-Baz

The prophet Isaiah gave his son this name, which means **"quick to the plunder, swift to the spoil."** It foretold the plunder of Samaria and its capital, Damascus, by the king of Assyria.

Isaiah 8:1-4

BALAAM'S DONKEY
ONLY ANIMAL TO TALK TO A PROPHET

It's true!

This one speaks for itself. Actually, **the Lord was speaking through the donkey** to warn Balaam of his reckless ways.

Numbers 22:21-31

EHUD
NINJA SKILLS

This crafty assassin killed the evil King Eglon of Moab by making his own sword and **sneaking it into the king's private chamber.** He escaped onto the porch and locked the doors to the king's room behind him. Those are some serious ninja skills.

Judges 3:15-30

OG'S BED

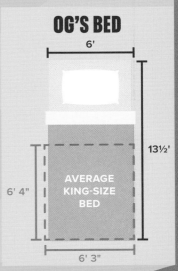

6'

13½'

6' 4"

AVERAGE KING-SIZE BED

6' 3"

OG
TALLEST PERSON

This king of Bashan was **between 10 and 13 feet tall.**

Deuteronomy 3:11

OG TOWERS ABOVE THE COMPETITION

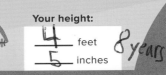

Og

Goliath • 9' 9"
Philistine warrior

Robert Wadlow • 8' 11"
The tallest man on record.

Sultan Kösen • 8' 3"
The tallest living man.

LeBron James • 6' 8"
One of the greatest basketball players of all time.

Your height:
4 feet 8 years
5 inches

DO-IT-ALL DAVID

A MAN AFTER GOD'S OWN HEART

SON

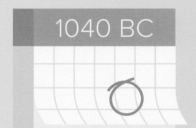
1040 BC

Born about 1040 BC

The youngest of 8 sons

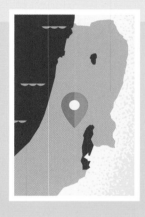
From Bethlehem (like Jesus)

WARRIOR

A stone could leave a sling in excess of 60 mph.

Defeated Goliath with a sling
(He was probably just a teenager!)

Conquered the Hittite city of Jerusalem
2 Samuel 5

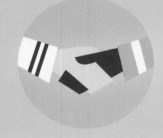
United the northern and southern factions of the kingdom of Israel

KING

Anointed by Samuel to be king

Reigned as king for 40 years
(starting when he was 30)
2 Samuel 5:4

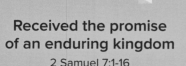
Received the promise of an enduring kingdom
2 Samuel 7:1-16

Played the lyre
(stringed instrument like
a U-shaped harp)

MUSICIAN

Worshipped God through
song and dance
2 Samuel 6:12-14

Author of about half
of the Psalms
(sacred songs)

SHEPHERD

GOOD-LOOKING

FRIEND

Tended father's sheep

Ruddy and handsome in appearance
1 Samuel 16:12

His bestie was King Saul's son
1 Samuel 18:1-5

FAMOUS

Had great success
in all he did

Loved by all of Israel
and Judah

Mentioned more than
1,100 times in the Bible

MAN OF GOD

Brought the Ark of the
Covenant to Jerusalem
2 Samuel 6

Chosen by God when Saul disobeyed
(Saul tried to kill David several times)

Man after God's own heart
1 Samuel 13:14

Although David was far from perfect, God said of him,
"I have found David...a man after my own heart" (Acts 13:22). Why?
Because David always admitted his mistakes and asked for forgiveness (Psalm 51).

Psalm (*noun*) : a song or hymn used in worship

PSALMS AND
PRAISES FOR GOD...

GET TO KNOW THE BOOK OF PSALMS

Psalm 117, with 2 verses, is the **shortest chapter** in the Bible.

Psalm 117 is the **middle chapter** in most English translations of the Bible.

Psalm 119, with **176 verses**, is the **longest chapter** in the Bible.

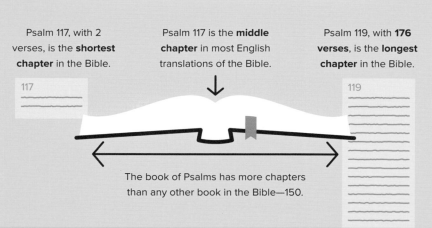

The book of Psalms has more chapters than any other book in the Bible—150.

THE PSALMS WERE WRITTEN BY...

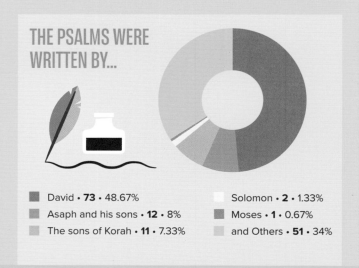

- David • **73** • 48.67%
- Asaph and his sons • **12** • 8%
- The sons of Korah • **11** • 7.33%
- Solomon • **2** • 1.33%
- Moses • **1** • 0.67%
- and Others • **51** • 34%

NAME THAT TUNE

Some popular songs are based on the psalms. Do these verses sound familiar?

"O LORD, our Lord, how majestic is Your name in all the earth!"
Psalm 8:1 NASB

"This is the day the LORD has made; we will rejoice and be glad in it."
Psalm 118:24 NKJV

"Bless the LORD, O my soul... bless His holy name"
Psalm 103:1 NASB

MUSICAL INSTRUMENTS IN PSALMS

HARP LYRE LUTE ZITHER CYMBALS

FLUTE PIPE TRUMPET SHOFAR TIMBREL
ram's horn tambourine

PSALMS AND PROVERBS
TOP 10

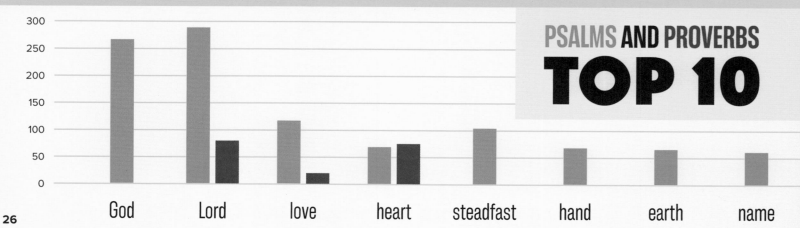

God   Lord   love   heart   steadfast   hand   earth   name

PROVERBS
...WISDOM FOR US

GETTING WISE ABOUT THE BOOK OF PROVERBS

The main author of Proverbs was Solomon, son of David. He was the third king of Israel and was **considered the wisest man** who had ever lived.

Other authors include...
Agur son of Jakeh
Lemuel (maybe another name for Solomon)
Possibly some of Solomon's wise men

NAME THAT PROVERB

These common sayings came from the book of Proverbs:

Iron sharpens iron
Proverbs 27:17

Sharp as a double-edged sword Proverbs 5:4

Heavy heart
Proverbs 25:20

Pride goes before a fall
Proverbs 16:18

Like snow in summer
Proverbs 26:1

OTHER SAYINGS BASED ON SCRIPTURE

A drop in the bucket
Isaiah 40:15

Don't throw your pearls before swine Matthew 7:6

Escape by the skin of one's teeth Job 19:20

Go the extra mile
Matthew 5:41

Together, **PSALMS** and **PROVERBS** contain tens of thousands of words. Looking at the **10 MOST-USED WORDS** from each book, we can see that **PSALMS** is focused on worshipping God, and **PROVERBS** provides wisdom and advice for people.

praise   soul   life   evil   wise   righteous   whoever   wicked   man

THE BOOK OF DANIEL
THE HUMBLE WILL BE EXALTED

GOD **EXALTS** THOSE WHO **HUMBLE** THEMSELVES IN HIS KINGDOM

Veggies and Water
Daniel 1

Daniel and his pals **reject the king's tasty food and wine** in obedience to God's law and opt for vegetables and water.

HUMBLED themselves

EXALTED by God

Ten days later, they are **stronger and healthier** than their peers who ate the king's food. King Nebuchadnezzar regarded them highly.

Fiery Furnace
Daniel 3

Shadrach, Meshach, and Abednego **refuse to obey the king's command** to bow before an image of gold and are thrown in a fiery furnace.

HUMBLED themselves

EXALTED by God

God protected them in the furnace. They are unharmed in the fire and are even given promotions!

Lions' Den
Daniel 6

Daniel continues to **talk to God** despite an order from the king not to pray to anyone but himself. Daniel is thrown into the den to become lion chow.

HUMBLED himself

EXALTED by God

Daniel emerges from the lions' den **without a scratch**, so the king issues a new decree to worship Daniel's God. Daniel prospers.

Teens in Training
Daniel was probably about 15 when he and his friends Shadrach, Meshach, and Abednego were taken to Babylon (about 605 BC).

Who Turned Up the Heat?
King Nebuchadnezzar was so mad at Daniel and his friends, he **heated the furnace seven times hotter than normal.** Taken literally, that would have made the furnace a whopping 11,000 degrees, or 1,000 degrees hotter than the surface of the sun!

Rough Stuff
A few licks from a lion's tongue could **take the skin off the back of your hand!**

humble (*adj*) : **lower** in dignity or importance

exalted (*verb*) : **raised** to a higher rank or a position of greater power

GOD **HUMBLES** THOSE WHO **EXALT** THEMSELVES IN HIS KINGDOM

Nebuchadnezzar's Dream of a Tree
Daniel 4

Nebuchadnezzar **boasted of his power, glory, and majesty** even though God warned him not to.

EXALTED himself

HUMBLED by God

The king refused to repent. He was **removed from power** and lived outside with the wild animals.

Belshazzar's Vision of Writing on the Wall
Daniel 5

King Belshazzar is warned that his days are numbered because he **refused to humble himself** before God.

EXALTED himself

HUMBLED by God

That very night, **he died**, for he had not learned from his grandfather's (Nebuchadnezzar's) mistakes.

Nebuchadnezzar's Dream of a Statue
Daniel 2

Daniel interprets the king's dream as a vision of the future. It shows how the kingdoms of the world will eventually all be **humbled** and God's kingdom will be **exalted**.

God Rewards a Humble Heart
After some time, Nebuchadnezzar **turned his eyes to heaven** and praised God.

HUMBLED himself

EXALTED by God

He was **restored to his throne** and became even greater than before.

Did You Know?
The mysterious hand wrote, *"Mene, Mene, Tekel, Parsin"* ("God has numbered the days of your reign and brought it to an end"). This is where we get the phrase, **"The writing is on the wall."**

The Hidden Power of Humility

The book of Daniel shows that when you humble yourself before God, He can use you for His kingdom in amazing ways!

CERTIFIED MIRACLE

GOD'S MIND-BLOWING MIRACLES

NAAMAN WASHES OFF HIS LEPROSY
in the muddy Jordan River
2 Kings 5:1-14

ELISHA makes an IRON AX-HEAD FLOAT in water
2 Kings 6:5-7

JESUS WALKS ON WATER
Matthew 14:22-33

JONAH survives three days in THE BELLY OF A GREAT FISH
Jonah 1:17–2:10

In Jonah's time, any aquatic creature could be referred to as a fish. Any of these species can swallow a man whole.

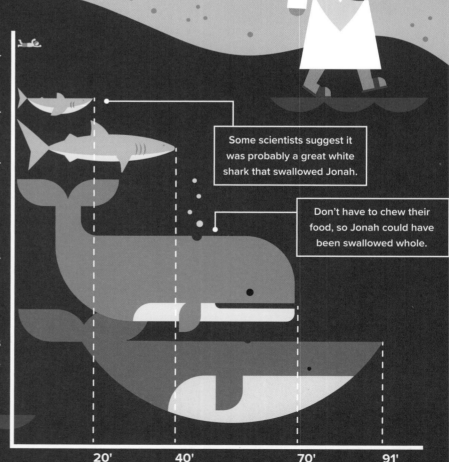

The average man
5' 9" • 196 lbs.

Great white sharks
20' long • 2,400 lbs.

Whale sharks
40' long • 41,000 lbs.

Sperm whales
70' long • 130,000 lbs.

Blue whales
91' long • 300,000 lbs.

Some scientists suggest it was probably a great white shark that swallowed Jonah.

Don't have to chew their food, so Jonah could have been swallowed whole.

20'   40'   70'   91'

THE SUN STANDS STILL for a full day so **JOSHUA** and his army can **WIN A BATTLE**
Joshua 10:12-14

ELIJAH is taken up to heaven in a **CHARIOT OF FIRE**
2 Kings 2:11

ELIJAH IS FED BREAD AND MEAT BY RAVENS in the wilderness
1 Kings 17:1-6

The average man needs at least **1,500 CALORIES A DAY JUST TO SURVIVE.** This is equal to about...

1 OR **3** OR **11** OR **14**

JESUS FEEDS THE 5,000
Matthew 14:15-21

This number included only men. The crowd could have been as large as **25,000** PEOPLE.

That's a lot of mouths to feed!

And there were 12 baskets left over!

If each person ate 2 fish, Jesus provided about **50,000** FISH

That's quite a seafood buffet!

Loaves were much smaller than they are today. If each person ate 3 loaves, Jesus provided about **75,000** LOAVES.

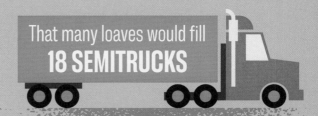

That many loaves would fill **18 SEMITRUCKS**

31

JESUS'S FAMILY TREE

JESUS IS Son of God, Son of Man, & Son of David ALL AT ONCE...HOW CAN THAT BE?

THROUGH MARY
LUKE 3:23-38

THROUGH JOSEPH
MATTHEW 1:1-17

ADAM

The first man.

Seth
Enosh
Kenan
Mahalalel
Jared
Enoch
Methuselah
Lamech

NOAH
2948–1998 BC
Only Noah and his family survived the great flood.

Shem
Arphaxad
Cainan
Shelah
Eber
Peleg
Reu
Serug
Nahor
Terah

JACOB
A star will come out of Jacob.
Numbers 24:17

ISAAC
Through Isaac's offspring, all will be reckoned to God.
Genesis 21:12

ABRAHAM
1996–1821 BC
Through Abraham's offspring, all nations will be blessed.
Genesis 22:18

JUDAH and TAMAR
The scepter will not depart from Judah.
Genesis 49:10

Perez
Hezron
Ram
Amminadab
Nahshon
Salmon and Rahab
Boaz and Ruth
Obed

JESSE
A shoot will come up from the stump of Jesse.
Isaiah 11:1

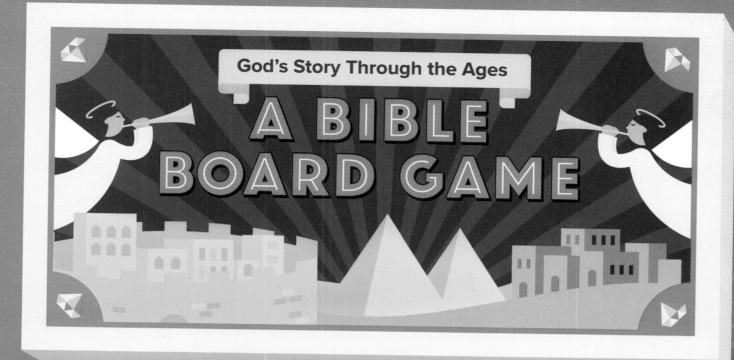

PLAY ALONG

SINGLE-PLAYER VERSION

Follow the timeline **WITHOUT DICE.**

Move **ONE SPACE AT A TIME,** following the grand story from beginning to end.

MULTI-PLAYER VERSION

Each player needs a **UNIQUE, SMALL OBJECT** for their game piece (like a coin).

The **OLDEST PLAYER** goes first.

ROLL ONE DIE and move your game piece the corresponding number of spaces.

KEEP TRACK of your points along the way.

Play until each player reaches the end of the game. Whoever has the **MOST POINTS, WINS!**

Ready? **LET'S PLAY!**

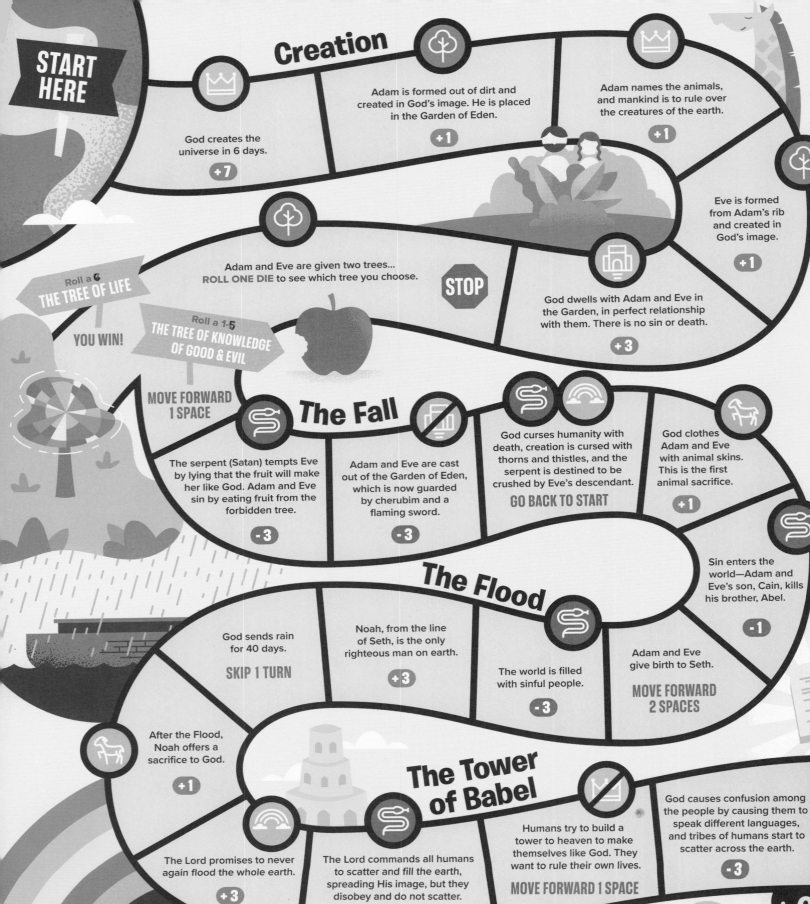

Creation

START HERE

God creates the universe in 6 days.
+7

Adam is formed out of dirt and created in God's image. He is placed in the Garden of Eden.
+1

Adam names the animals, and mankind is to rule over the creatures of the earth.
+1

Eve is formed from Adam's rib and created in God's image.
+1

Adam and Eve are given two trees...
ROLL ONE DIE to see which tree you choose.

STOP

God dwells with Adam and Eve in the Garden, in perfect relationship with them. There is no sin or death.
+3

Roll a 6
THE TREE OF LIFE
YOU WIN!

Roll a 1-5
THE TREE OF KNOWLEDGE OF GOOD & EVIL
MOVE FORWARD 1 SPACE

The Fall

The serpent (Satan) tempts Eve by lying that the fruit will make her like God. Adam and Eve sin by eating fruit from the forbidden tree.
-3

Adam and Eve are cast out of the Garden of Eden, which is now guarded by cherubim and a flaming sword.
-3

God curses humanity with death, creation is cursed with thorns and thistles, and the serpent is destined to be crushed by Eve's descendant.
GO BACK TO START

God clothes Adam and Eve with animal skins. This is the first animal sacrifice.
+1

Sin enters the world—Adam and Eve's son, Cain, kills his brother, Abel.
-1

The Flood

God sends rain for 40 days.
SKIP 1 TURN

Noah, from the line of Seth, is the only righteous man on earth.
+3

The world is filled with sinful people.
-3

Adam and Eve give birth to Seth.
MOVE FORWARD 2 SPACES

After the Flood, Noah offers a sacrifice to God.
+1

The Lord promises to never again flood the whole earth.
+3

The Lord commands all humans to scatter and fill the earth, spreading His image, but they disobey and do not scatter.
-1

The Tower of Babel

Humans try to build a tower to heaven to make themselves like God. They want to rule their own lives.
MOVE FORWARD 1 SPACE

God causes confusion among the people by causing them to speak different languages, and tribes of humans start to scatter across the earth.
-3

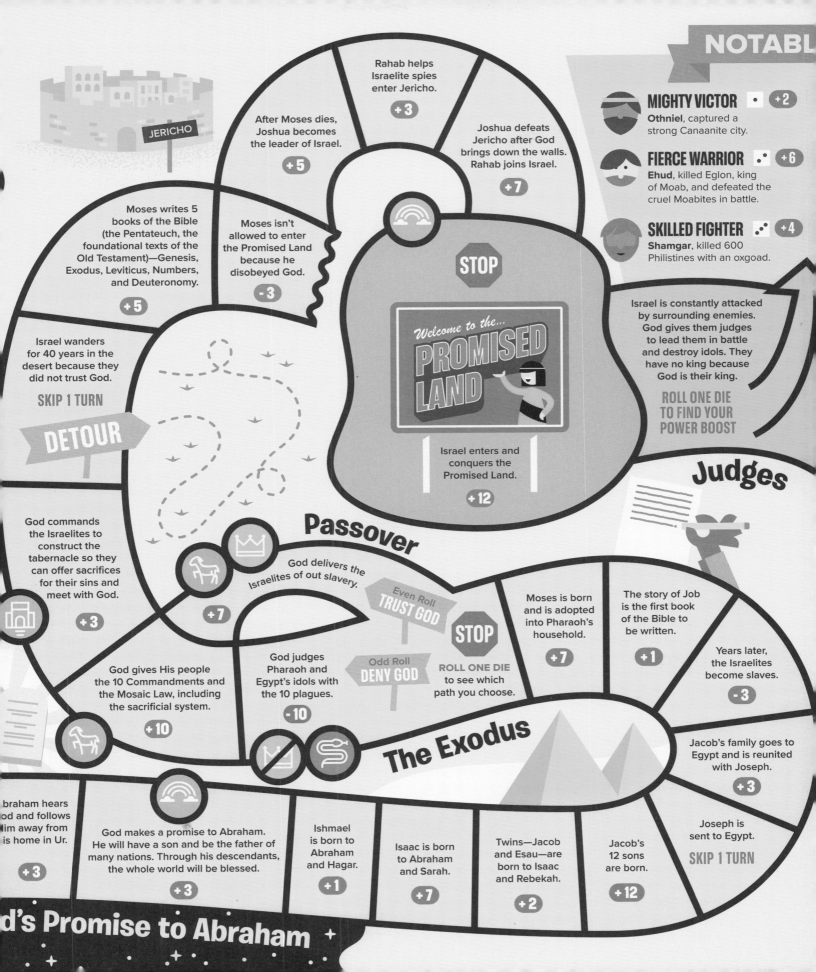

JERICHO

Rahab helps Israelite spies enter Jericho.
+3

After Moses dies, Joshua becomes the leader of Israel.
+5

Joshua defeats Jericho after God brings down the walls. Rahab joins Israel.
+7

Moses writes 5 books of the Bible (the Pentateuch, the foundational texts of the Old Testament)—Genesis, Exodus, Leviticus, Numbers, and Deuteronomy.
+5

Moses isn't allowed to enter the Promised Land because he disobeyed God.
-3

STOP

Welcome to the...
PROMISED LAND

Israel enters and conquers the Promised Land.
+12

Israel wanders for 40 years in the desert because they did not trust God.
SKIP 1 TURN

DETOUR

NOTABL

MIGHTY VICTOR · **+2**
Othniel, captured a strong Canaanite city.

FIERCE WARRIOR ∴ **+6**
Ehud, killed Eglon, king of Moab, and defeated the cruel Moabites in battle.

SKILLED FIGHTER ∷ **+4**
Shamgar, killed 600 Philistines with an oxgoad.

Israel is constantly attacked by surrounding enemies. God gives them judges to lead them in battle and destroy idols. They have no king because God is their king.
ROLL ONE DIE TO FIND YOUR POWER BOOST

Judges

God commands the Israelites to construct the tabernacle so they can offer sacrifices for their sins and meet with God.
+3

Passover

God delivers the Israelites of out slavery.
+7

God gives His people the 10 Commandments and the Mosaic Law, including the sacrificial system.
+10

God judges Pharaoh and Egypt's idols with the 10 plagues.
-10

Even Roll TRUST GOD

Odd Roll DENY GOD

STOP
ROLL ONE DIE to see which path you choose.

Moses is born and is adopted into Pharaoh's household.
+7

The story of Job is the first book of the Bible to be written.
+1

Years later, the Israelites become slaves.
-3

The Exodus

Jacob's family goes to Egypt and is reunited with Joseph.
+3

Joseph is sent to Egypt.
SKIP 1 TURN

braham hears od and follows im away from is home in Ur.
+3

God makes a promise to Abraham. He will have a son and be the father of many nations. Through his descendants, the whole world will be blessed.
+3

Ishmael is born to Abraham and Hagar.
+1

Isaac is born to Abraham and Sarah.
+7

Twins—Jacob and Esau—are born to Isaac and Rebekah.
+2

Jacob's 12 sons are born.
+12

d's Promise to Abraham

JEHOIACHIN

Born in 615 or 605 BC

Dethroned and captured by Babylon in 586 or 587 BC.

None of Jehoiachin's offspring will prosper, none will sit on the throne of David or rule in Judah. Jeremiah 22:24-30

This means the Savior can't be a PHYSICAL descendant of David from Joseph's line.

Shealtiel
Zerubbabel
Abihud
Eliakim
Azor

Jacob
Matthan
Eleazar
Elihud
Akim
Zadok

JOSEPH

90 BC–18 AD

Because of the curse on Jehoiachin, no PHYSICAL relative of Joseph can sit on David's throne, but Jesus isn't the PHYSICAL son of Joseph. He's ADOPTED.

Jesus's LEGAL right to David's throne, which can come only from the father's lineage, is fulfilled through Joseph.

GOD KEEPS ALL HIS PROMISES

Through the virgin birth, God kept His promise to David that the Savior would be a blood relative, even though Joseph's side of David's family tree was cursed. None of these men and women were perfect, but God used them to bring us a perfect Savior.

Josiah
Amon
Manasseh
Hezekiah
Ahaz
Jotham
Uzziah
Jehoram
Asa
Abijah
Rehoboam

JESUS

4 BC–30 or 33 AD

JESUS IS THE SON OF GOD
Fulfilled by the virgin conception
Luke 1:34-35

JESUS IS THE SON OF MAN
Fulfilled through Mary and born as a human

JESUS IS THE SON OF DAVID
Fulfilled through Joseph

Neri
Melki
Addi
Cosam
Elmadam
Er
Joshua
Eliezer
Jorim
Matthat
Levi
Simeon
Judah
Joseph
Jonam
Eliakim
Melea
Menna
Mattatha
Nathan

Shealtiel
Zerubbabel
Rhesa
Joanan
Joda
Josek
Semein
Mattathias
Maath
Naggai
Esli
Nahum
Amos
Mattathias
Joseph
Jannai
Melchi
Levi
Matthat
Heli

SOLOMON

1010–931 BC

Solomon's throne will be established forever.
1 Chronicles 22:9-10

MARY

18 BC–48 AD

The virgin will conceive and give birth to a son, and will call him Immanuel.
Isaiah 7:14

Jesus fulfills His PHYSICAL right to David's throne through Mary.

DAVID and BATHSHEBA

1085–1015 BC

David's throne will be established forever.
2 Samuel 7:12-16

THEMES

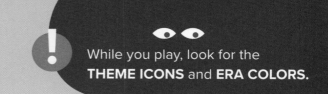
While you play, look for the
THEME ICONS and **ERA COLORS.**

 God brings NEW LIFE

 GOD REIGNS as King

 GOD REJECTED as King

 SATAN'S OPPOSITION to God and our rebellion

SATAN and SIN DEFEATED

 CHRIST'S REDEMPTION of mankind through His sacrifice

 GOD DWELLS with HUMANITY

 Our relationship with God HINDERED BY OUR SIN

 GOD'S PROMISES

 THE FEAR that God's promises MAY NOT COME TRUE

ERAS

The Beginning
God creates the universe and mankind. Mankind rebels against God.

The Birth of Israel
God forms a new nation from Abraham to bless the world.

The Era of Kings
God's nation rebels against Him, rejecting Him as king. Israel's own kings lead them astray.

The New Testament
God sends Jesus, His own Son, to die for the world to save us from our sin.

35

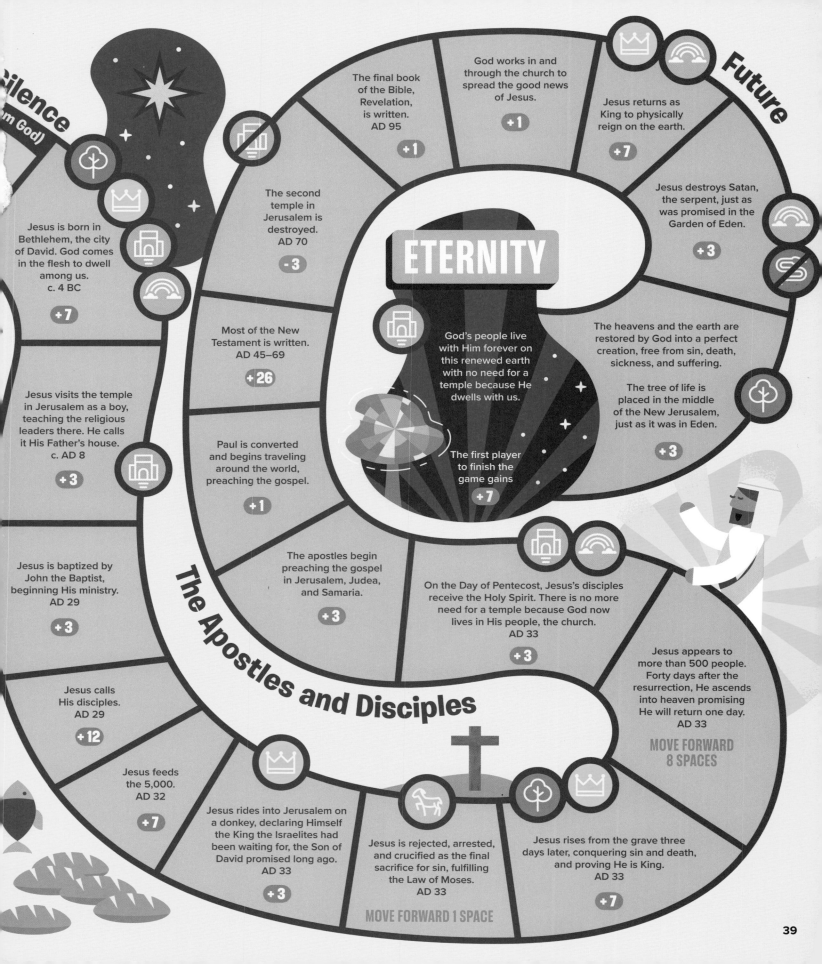

Silence
(from God)

The final book of the Bible, Revelation, is written. AD 95
+1

God works in and through the church to spread the good news of Jesus.
+1

Future

Jesus returns as King to physically reign on the earth.
+7

The second temple in Jerusalem is destroyed. AD 70
- 3

Jesus destroys Satan, the serpent, just as was promised in the Garden of Eden.
+3

Jesus is born in Bethlehem, the city of David. God comes in the flesh to dwell among us. c. 4 BC
+7

ETERNITY

God's people live with Him forever on this renewed earth with no need for a temple because He dwells with us.

The heavens and the earth are restored by God into a perfect creation, free from sin, death, sickness, and suffering.

Most of the New Testament is written. AD 45–69
+26

The tree of life is placed in the middle of the New Jerusalem, just as it was in Eden.
+3

Jesus visits the temple in Jerusalem as a boy, teaching the religious leaders there. He calls it His Father's house. c. AD 8
+3

Paul is converted and begins traveling around the world, preaching the gospel.
+1

The first player to finish the game gains
+7

The Apostles and Disciples

Jesus is baptized by John the Baptist, beginning His ministry. AD 29
+3

The apostles begin preaching the gospel in Jerusalem, Judea, and Samaria.
+3

On the Day of Pentecost, Jesus's disciples receive the Holy Spirit. There is no more need for a temple because God now lives in His people, the church. AD 33
+3

Jesus appears to more than 500 people. Forty days after the resurrection, He ascends into heaven promising He will return one day. AD 33

MOVE FORWARD 8 SPACES

Jesus calls His disciples. AD 29
+12

Jesus feeds the 5,000. AD 32
+7

Jesus rides into Jerusalem on a donkey, declaring Himself the King the Israelites had been waiting for, the Son of David promised long ago. AD 33
+3

Jesus is rejected, arrested, and crucified as the final sacrifice for sin, fulfilling the Law of Moses. AD 33

MOVE FORWARD 1 SPACE

Jesus rises from the grave three days later, conquering sin and death, and proving He is King. AD 33
+7

JUDGES

COURAGOUS LEADER :: +10
Deborah, prophetess who urged Barak to lead an army to defeat Sisera's troops.

SUPER STRENGTH :: +12
Samson, killed 1,000 Philistines with a donkey's jawbone and tore down their temple while blinded.

GRAND CHAMPION :: +8
Gideon, defeated 135,000 Midianites with only 300 men.

Malachi, the last Old Testament prophet, prophesies of a coming messenger from the Lord. 433–424 BC
MOVE FORWARD 4 SPACES

Roman rule over Israel begins. 63 BC
SKIP 4 TURNS

Esther marries King Xerxes and becomes queen of the Persian Empire.
+3

The new temple is finished. The Israelites finally have a place to offer sacrifices and meet with God again. 516 BC
+3

Elisha prophesies to evil northern kings Joram (c. 852–841), Jehu (c. 841–814 BC), Jehoahaz (c. 814–798), and Jehoash (c. 798–782 BC).
-3

Elijah prophesies to evil northern kings Ahab (c. 874–853 BC) and Ahaziah (c. 853–852 BC).
-3

The Life of Jesus

A temple in Jerusalem is destroyed. The Israelites no longer have a physical place to offer sacrifices and meet with God. They have no king to fulfill the promise made to David.
-3

Jeroboam becomes king of Israel. c. 931 BC
-300

The Exile

Daniel is carried off to Babylon. 597 BC
-1

Jonah prophesies to Nineveh in Assyria. c. 780–775 BC
SKIP 1 TURN

Even Roll
THE NORTHERN KINGDOM: ISRAEL (10 tribes)

Ruth, a Moabite widow, follows her Israelite mother-in-law to Bethlehem. Ruth marries Boaz and becomes the great-grandmother of King David.
MOVE FORWARD 3 SPACES

The Babylonian Empire takes the southern kingdom captive. 605 BC
-3

The Assyrian Empire takes the northern kingdom captive. 722 BC
-3

The Kingdom Is Divided

ROLL ONE DIE to see which path you take, and move that many spaces.

STOP

The Israelites reject God as king and demand a human king. Samuel crowns Saul as the first king of Israel. c. 1043 BC
-1

Josiah becomes king of the southern kingdom at 8 years old.
+3

Isaiah prophesies during the reigns of four kings.
+3

Odd Roll
THE SOUTHERN KINGDOM: JUDAH (Judah & Benjamin)

Israel is split into two kingdoms.

David replaces Saul as king. c. 1013 BC
+1

God promises David that one of his descendants will rule forever.
+3

Solomon, David's son, builds the temple so the Israelites can have a permanent place to offer sacrifices to God and meet with Him.
+3

Solomon sins and falls into idolatry.
-1

Rehoboam succeeds Solomon as king. c. 931 BC
MOVE FORWARD 1 SPACE

The kingdom revolts against Rehoboam because he is a bad king. c. 931 BC
-3

The Kingdom Is United

BEHOLD, A CHILD IS BORN!

EXPLORING THE NATIVITY SCENE
Matthew 2; Luke 2

THE NATIVITY SCENE as we know it first appeared in **AD 1223** when Saint Francis of Assisi was given permission to stage the scene in a cave.

SHEPHERDS

- The shepherds were out in their field when the angel spoke to them, so Jesus was most likely born in the **LATE SUMMER** or early fall, not in December.
- They saw Jesus shortly after He was born. He was lying in a manger.

STABLE

- It is assumed that Jesus was born in a stable because He was placed in a manger.
- This was possibly the lower floor of a house where some animals were brought inside.

ANIMALS

- Jesus was placed in a manger, so animals could have been present.

MANGER

manger (*noun*) : a trough or open box in a stable to hold food for livestock

- It reminds us that Jesus is our **SPIRITUAL FOOD** (John 6:35).
- It was made from clay mixed with straw, or built with stones and mud, or carved in rock.

STAR OF BETHLEHEM

- A star appeared that would eventually **LEAD THE WISE MEN TO BETHLEHEM.**
- Some theories say the "star" could have been a comet or the alignment of Jupiter and Venus. Regardless, it was indeed miraculous.

CERTIFIED MIRACLE

JESUS

JESUS'S BIRTH MARKS THE CHANGE IN THE CALENDAR

← BC "Before Christ"	AD "*anno Domini*," Medieval Latin for "in the year of the Lord" →

- Jesus's birthday was possibly as early as **5 BC.**
- On the eighth day, He was named Jesus, meaning **"THE LORD SAVES."**
- The Western church picked **DECEMBER 25** as Jesus's birthday, and the Eastern church picked **JANUARY 6.** Eventually this season became known as the **12 DAYS OF CHRISTMAS.**
- In Greek, "X", or *chi*, is the first letter of Christ's name, and it became a well-known symbol for Christ. Therefore, **"XMAS"** is another way to write "Christmas."

WISE MEN

magi (*noun*) : astrologers and interpreters

- The wise men visited Jesus when He was a toddler, not a newborn.
- It is not known how many wise men were actually there. Because **3 GIFTS** are mentioned, tradition says there were **3 VISITORS.**

 Gold
a valuable metal to signify His kingship on earth

 Frankincense
a fragrant perfume to signify His priestly role on earth

 Myrrh
an anointing oil to signify His death and resurrection

MARY & JOSEPH

- **TRAVELED 70 MILES** from Nazareth to Bethlehem for the Roman census, about a 1-hour car ride for us. For them, it was a **3-DAY JOURNEY ON FOOT...** and Mary was 9 months pregnant!
- **MARY GAVE BIRTH IN BETHLEHEM** (as prophesied in Micah 5:2) during the time of Herod the Great.

Nazareth

Jerusalem
Bethlehem

HEROD WHO?

 Herod the Great
The king who enlarged the Jewish temple and who died shortly after Jesus's birth.

 Herod Antipas
The king during the life and death of Jesus and the one who killed John the Baptist.

 Herod Agrippa I
Herod the Great's grandson, the king who killed the apostle James and imprisoned Peter.

THE BIBLE CALLED IT ✓ JESUS FULFILLED IT

Depending on how you count, **Jesus fulfilled over 150 prophecies from the Bible.** He did *everything* the Bible said He would! Here's just a small fraction of the prophecies that Jesus fulfilled in His birth, life, ministry, death, and resurrection:

Prophecy (*noun*) : a prediction of what's to come

Descendant of Abraham
Genesis 12:3; 17:17,19

Matthew 1:1-2,16; Luke 3:23,34 ✓

Descendant of David
2 Samuel 7:12-16; Isaiah 9:6-7

Luke 1:32 ✓

Born in Bethlehem
Micah 5:2

Luke 2:4-7 ✓

Born of a virgin
Isaiah 7:13-14

Luke 1:26-31 ✓

Flees to Egypt
Hosea 11:1

Matthew 2:13-15 ✓

Follows a messenger
Isaiah 40:3

Matthew 3:1-3 ✓

Teaches in parables
Psalm 78:1-2

Matthew 13:34-35 ✓

Rides into Jerusalem on a donkey
Zechariah 9:9

Matthew 21:1-11 ✓

Parable (*noun*) : short story used to teach a spiritual lesson

Betrayed by a close friend who eats with Him
Psalm 41:9

John 13:18 ✓

Side is pierced
Zechariah 12:10

John 19:34

Hands and feet are pierced
Psalm 22:15-16

John 20:25-27

No bones are broken
Exodus 12:43-46; Psalm 34:19-20

John 19:33-36

Rises from the dead (hallelujah!)
Psalm 16:10-11; 49:15

Mark 16:5-6

Ascends to heaven and sits at God's right hand
Psalm 68:18

Acts 1:9; 2:32-33; 1 Corinthians 15:3-4

WHAT ARE THE ODDS?

THE ODDS OF

1 PERSON FULLFILLING **8 PROPHECIES**

WOULD BE

1 in **100,000,000,000,000,000**

That's ONE in "a hundred quadrillion"!

THAT MANY SILVER DOLLARS WOULD COVER THE STATE OF TEXAS TWO FEET DEEP

THAT'S THE SAME ODDS AS SOMEONE FINDING ONE SPECIFIC COIN ON THEIR FIRST TRY

2 FEET

Adapted from Josh McDowell's
Evidence That Demands a Verdict

THE ODDS OF

1 PERSON FULLFILLING **48 PROPHECIES**

WOULD BE

1 in **10,000,000,000,000,000,
000,000,000,000,000,000,000,
000,000,000,000,000,000,000,
000,000,000,000,000,000,000,
000,000,000,000,000,000,000,
000,000,000,000,000,000,000,
000,000,000,000,000,000,000,
000,000,000,000,000**

That's the estimated **NUMBER** of **STARS** in **OUR UNIVERSE**!

And **Jesus fulfilled far more than 48 prophesies.**
We're gonna need more zeros here!

JESUS IS CRUCIFIED
SACRIFICED FOR OUR SIN

Legend
- Time when event occured
- Prophesy
- ✓ Fulfilled
- |————————| .25 miles

THE VIA DOLOROSA, or "the way of suffering," was about a third of a mile long. **Normally a 9-minute walk, it took Jesus 3 hours.**

Calvary (Latin) and *Golgotha* (Hebrew) mean **"a skull."**

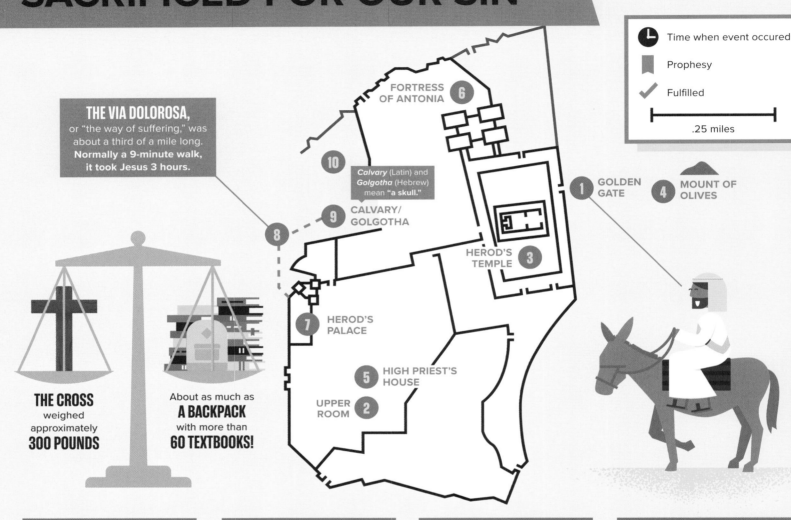

Map locations:
- FORTRESS OF ANTONIA — 6
- 10
- 9 CALVARY/GOLGOTHA
- 8
- HEROD'S TEMPLE — 3
- 1 GOLDEN GATE
- 4 MOUNT OF OLIVES
- 7 HEROD'S PALACE
- 5 HIGH PRIEST'S HOUSE
- UPPER ROOM — 2

THE CROSS weighed approximately **300 POUNDS**

About as much as **A BACKPACK** with more than **60 TEXTBOOKS!**

---

1 RODE INTO JERUSALEM ON PALM SUNDAY.

JESUS RODE ON A DONKEY	
▌ Zechariah 9:9	Matthew 21:5-6 ✓

 A week before the resurrection.

2 SHARED THE LAST SUPPER WITH DISCIPLES.

 The day before the crucifixion.

3 BETRAYED BY JUDAS, ONE OF HIS 12 DISCIPLES.

HE WAS BETRAYED BY A FRIEND	
▌ Psalm 55:12-14	Matthew 26:48-50 ✓

JUDAS WAS PAID 30 PIECES OF SILVER	
▌ Zechariah 11:12	Matthew 26:14-15 ✓

4 ARRESTED BY A CROWD IN THE MIDDLE OF THE NIGHT.

HIS DISCIPLES DESERTED HIM	
▌ Zechariah 13:7	Matthew 26:56 ✓

5 TRIED BEFORE THE SANHEDRIN.

HE WAS ACCUSED BY FALSE WITNESSES	
▌ Psalm 35:11	Matthew 26:59-60 ✓

6 TRIED BEFORE PONTIUS PILATE.

HE WAS SILENT BEFORE HIS ACCUSERS	
▌ Isaiah 53:7	Matthew 27:12-14 ✓

7 SENTENCED TO DEATH BY PILATE.

HE WAS SPIT UPON	
▌ Isaiah 50:6	Matthew 27:30 ✓

8 CARRIED THE CROSS TO CALVARY.

9 JESUS IS HUNG ON THE CROSS.

🕘 **9 a.m.**   🕛 **12 p.m.**   🕒 **3 p.m.**

9 a.m.

CRUCIFIED WITH CRIMINALS

📑 Isaiah 53:12   **Mark 15:27-28** ✓

PARDONED THIEF ON THE CROSS — Luke 23:42-43

PRAYED FOR HIS PERSECUTORS

📑 Isaiah 53:12   **Luke 23:34** ✓

SOLDIERS GAMBLED FOR HIS CLOTHING

📑 Psalm 22:18   **Matthew 27:35** ✓

SPOKE TO HIS MOTHER AND JOHN — John 19:26-27

They were also joined by:
Mary Magdalene, Mary (mother of
James and Joseph), and Mary (wife of
Clopas, mother of the sons of Zebedee).

CRIED OUT FOR THIRST — John 19:28

GIVEN WINE VINEGAR TO DRINK

📑 Psalm 69:21   **John 19:29-30** ✓

12 p.m.

DARKNESS FELL OVER ALL THE LAND

📑 Amos 8:9   **Matthew 27:45** ✓

Darkness had preceded judgment
before—see 9th plague on page 15.

CRIED OUT, "MY GOD, MY GOD WHY HAVE YOU FORSAKEN ME?"

📑 Psalm 22:1   **Matthew 27:46** ✓

HE PRAYED, "INTO YOUR HANDS I COMMIT MY SPIRIT"

📑 Psalm 31:5   **Luke 23:46** ✓

This was a common Jewish phrase
recited before bedtime, almost as if saying,
"I trust You will wake me up tomorrow."
It foreshadows Jesus's resurrection.

The massive veil was
4 INCHES THICK
and so strong a
PAIR OF HORSES*
couldn't tear it apart!

60'

30'

*Horses not
to scale.

3 p.m.

CALLED OUT, "IT IS FINISHED" — John 19:29-30

HIS BONES WERE NOT BROKEN

📑 Psalm 34:20   **John 19:33** ✓

HIS SIDE WAS PIERCED

📑 Zechariah 12:10   **John 19:34-37** ✓

HIS LIFE IS POURED OUT

📑 Psalm 22:14   **John 19:34** ✓

THERE WAS A GREAT EARTHQUAKE — Matthew 27:51

**GRAVES OPENED, AND PEOPLE WERE RAISED
FROM THE DEAD** — Matthew 27:52-53

A CENTURION FOUND FAITH — Luke 23:47

A centurion was the commander
of 80 or 160 Roman soldiers.

THE TEMPLE VEIL WAS TORN — Matthew 27:51

The veil had separated the Most Holy
Place from the rest of the temple. God's
presence was now accessible to all.

10 JESUS IS BURIED IN A TOMB.

BURIED IN A RICH MAN'S TOMB

📑 Isaiah 53:9   **Matthew 27:57-60** ✓

Tomb (*noun*) :
an enclosure for a
corpse cut in the
earth or in rock

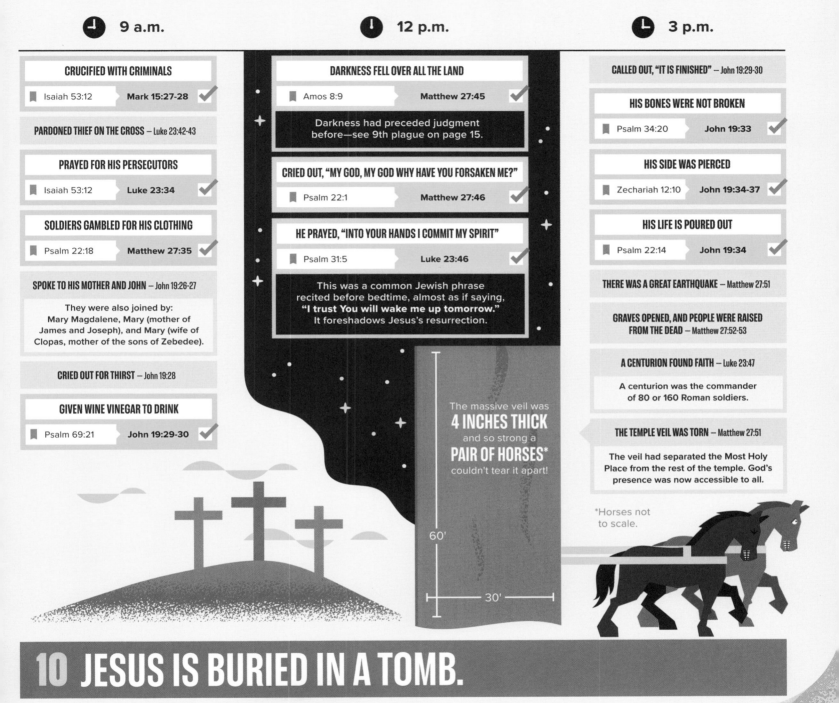

HALLELUJAH

JESUS WAS BURIED IN A TOMB

The tomb was guarded by at least four Roman soldiers and was closed with a special seal that could be broken only upon penalty of death.

The stone was four to six feet across and a foot thick. It weighed about **3,000 pounds**—as much as a small car.

HE SPENT 3 DAYS IN THE TOMB

ON THE THIRD DAY THERE WAS A

VIOLENT EARTHQUAKE.
An angel of the Lord rolled the stone away from the tomb's entrance and sat on it.

THIS TERRIFIED THE ROMAN SOLDIERS guarding the tomb. They were told by the chief priests to say that Jesus's disciples came in the night and stole His body while the soldiers were sleeping.

3 IS NOT A RANDOM NUMBER

There were
3 DIVISIONS
in the **tabernacle**.
Check it out on page 19.

1	2	3

Jonah spent
3 DAYS
in the belly of a fish.
Matthew 12:40

Jesus waited at least
3 DAYS
to raise **Lazarus from the dead.**
John 11:38-44

Lazarus...

It was customary to wait
3 DAYS
in Jewish culture to make sure a deceased person was actually dead. This way people knew they had seen a **true miracle**.

1 2 3

HE IS RISEN!

Matthew 27–28
Luke 24
John 20

JESUS APPEARED FOR 40 DAYS AFTER HIS RESURRECTION

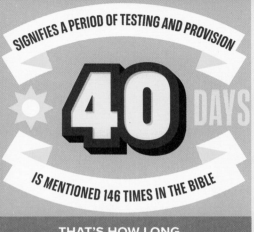

SIGNIFIES A PERIOD OF TESTING AND PROVISION

40 DAYS

IS MENTIONED 146 TIMES IN THE BIBLE

THAT'S HOW LONG...

it rained during the flood
Genesis 7:4,12

Moses was on Mount Sinai with God
Exodus 34:28

the spies explored the Promised Land
Numbers 13:25

Jonah said the Ninevites had to repent
Jonah 3:4

Jesus fasted and was tempted by the devil
Matthew 4:1-11

JESUS APPEARED TO MANY AFTER HIS RESURRECTION, INCLUDING...

James, near Damascus
1 Corinthians 15:7

Mary Magdalene, outside the tomb
John 20:14-16

Saul, on the road to Damascus
Acts 9:3-5

Cleopas and a companion, on the road to Emmaus
Luke 24:13-32

Simon Peter, in Jerusalem
Luke 24:34

Mary the mother of James, Salome, and Joanna
Mark 16:1; Luke 24:10

All the disciples
John 20:26

More than 500 people, in Galilee
1 Corinthians 15:6

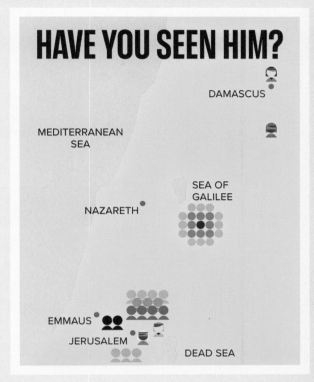

HAVE YOU SEEN HIM?

DAMASCUS

MEDITERRANEAN SEA

NAZARETH

SEA OF GALILEE

EMMAUS

JERUSALEM

DEAD SEA

THE SIGNIFICANCE OF THE RESURRECTION WAS MAJOR

For example, it...

broke the power of sin and death

displayed Christ's power to forgive sin

fulfilled prophecies about the Messiah

sets Christianity apart from other religions

Which religions believe...	Christianity	Judaism	Islam	Baha'i	Hinduism	Buddhism	New Age
in no gods						✓	✓
in other gods					✓		
in one God	✓	✓	✓	✓			
in the Trinity	✓						
Jesus was Mary's son	✓	✓	✓	✓			
Jesus was born of a virgin	✓		✓	✓			
Jesus was a wise man	✓	✓	✓	✓	✓	✓	✓
Jesus was divine	✓		✓	✓	✓	✓	
Jesus was the Messiah	✓						
Jesus died on the cross	✓	✓		✓			
Jesus was resurrected	✓						

Error

47

JESUS'S 12 DISCIPLES

• ORDINARY MEN, EXTRAORDINARY CALLING •

disciple (*noun*)
1 : a student
2 : a follower of Christ
3 : one of Christ's 12 closest followers in the Gospels

OCCUPATION KEY

 Fisherman

Tax Collector

 Unknown

Simon (Peter)

Leader of the 12 disciples
(Fisherman)

Andrew

Originally a disciple of John the Baptist
(Fisherman)

James

"James the Elder"
(Fisherman)

John

"The beloved disciple"
(Fisherman)

Philip

Led Nathaniel to Jesus
(Fisherman)

Nathaniel (Bartholomew)

A descendant of David
(Unknown)

Matthew (Levi)

His Gospel appears first in our New Testament
(Tax Collector)

James

"James the Younger"
(Unknown)

Judas

Also called Jude, Thaddeus, or Lebbeus
(Unknown)

Simon the Zealot

Zealot (*noun*) : extremist
(Fisherman)

Thomas

Doubted Jesus's resurrection at first
(Unknown)

Judas Iscariot

Betrayed Jesus
(Unknown)

Matthias

Chosen to replace Judas
(Unknown)

JESUS TEACHES HIS DISCIPLES

- **He began His ministry** around the age of 30, typical for rabbis (teachers) of that time.

- **He didn't teach only in synagogues.** He taught outdoors, on roads and seashores and mountaintops. **His message was considered radical** by most of the Jewish leaders of His time.

- **His 12 disciples** lived with Him, ate with Him, and went everywhere with Him. They could have been teenagers when Jesus called them—except for Peter, who was older.

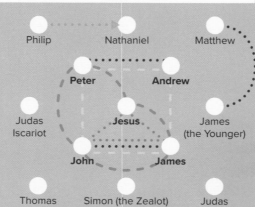

THE DISCIPLES' CONNECTIONS

• • • Brothers
• • • Cousins
– – Jesus's three closest friends
• • • Brought to Jesus
– – Worked Together

Philip   Nathaniel   Matthew

Peter   Andrew

Judas Iscariot   Jesus   James (the Younger)

John   James

Thomas   Simon (the Zealot)   Judas

AUTHORS INSPIRED BY JESUS

The New Testament has **9 authors**, including **3 of the 12 disciples.**

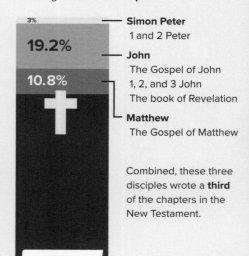

3%

19.2%

10.8%

Simon Peter
1 and 2 Peter

John
The Gospel of John
1, 2, and 3 John
The book of Revelation

Matthew
The Gospel of Matthew

Combined, these three disciples wrote a **third** of the chapters in the New Testament.

THE DISCIPLES WERE ALSO CALLED APOSTLES

apostle (noun)
1 : one sent on a mission, such as those sent out to preach the gospel
2 : one of Christ's 12 original disciples

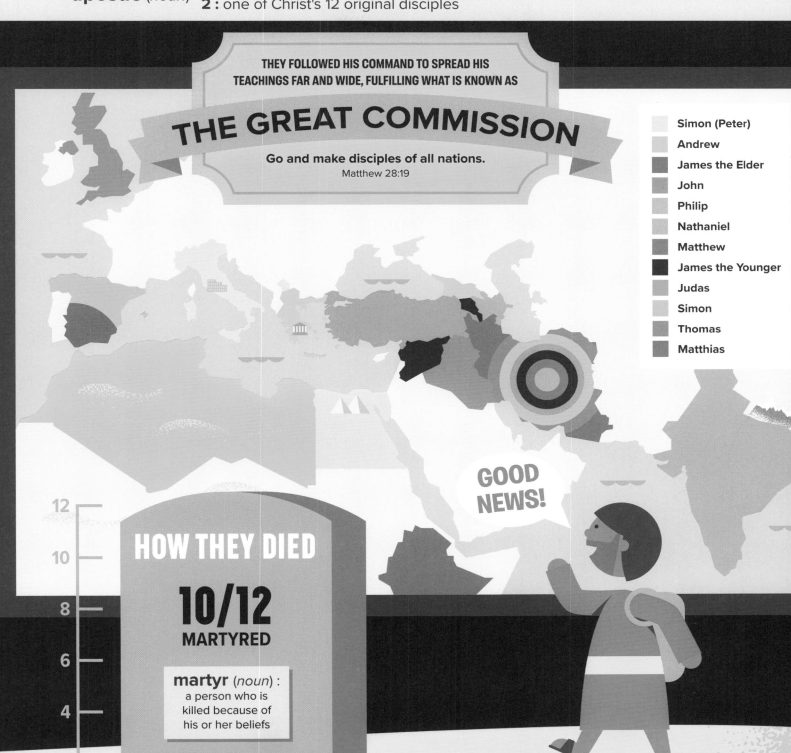

THEY FOLLOWED HIS COMMAND TO SPREAD HIS
TEACHINGS FAR AND WIDE, FULFILLING WHAT IS KNOWN AS

THE GREAT COMMISSION

Go and make disciples of all nations.
Matthew 28:19

- Simon (Peter)
- Andrew
- James the Elder
- John
- Philip
- Nathaniel
- Matthew
- James the Younger
- Judas
- Simon
- Thomas
- Matthias

GOOD NEWS!

HOW THEY DIED

10/12
MARTYRED

martyr (noun) :
a person who is
killed because of
his or her beliefs

John died of old age.

Judas, after betraying Jesus,
sadly chose to end his own life.

THE APOSTLE PAUL

WHO WAS PAUL?

- Also called Saul
- Roman citizen
- Tentmaker
- Jew from the tribe of Benjamin
- Pharisee

pharisee (*noun*) :
a member of a Jewish sect that followed the law and tradition very strictly

- **Zealous** (both as a persecutor of Christians and later as an apostle of Jesus Christ)

zealous (*adjective*) :
filled with passion for a person, a cause, or an ideal

- **Persecutor of Christians**
- **Christian Convert**—Acts 9

- **Apostle**
- **Author**

WHAT DID PAUL WRITE?

He wrote almost half of the books in the New Testament.

Paul's New Testament writings were actually epistles to churches or individuals.

epistle (*noun*) : a letter

Prison epistles—written while Paul was in jail.

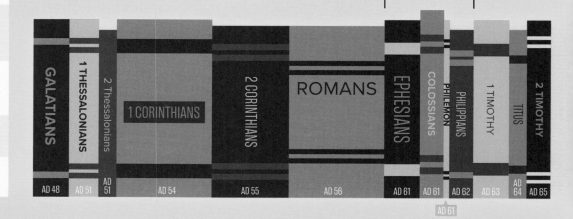

GALATIANS — AD 48
1 THESSALONIANS — AD 51
2 Thessalonians — AD 51
1 CORINTHIANS — AD 54
2 CORINTHIANS — AD 55
ROMANS — AD 56
EPHESIANS — AD 61
COLOSSIANS — AD 61
PHILEMON — AD 61
PHILIPPIANS — AD 62
1 TIMOTHY — AD 63
TITUS — AD 64
2 TIMOTHY — AD 65

PAUL'S PERSEVERANCE 2 CORINTHIANS 11:23-26

 6 YEARS SPENT IN PRISON
He shared the gospel with prisoners, guards, and even his accusers, and he wrote several epistles.

 3 TIMES SHIPWRECKED

 1 TIME BITTEN BY A SNAKE
Paul was unharmed and shared the gospel with the people on the island of Malta.

 **5 TIMES LASHED 40 MINUS 1**
39 was the maximum number allowed in order to prevent death by whipping.

 3 TIMES BEATEN WITH RODS

 **1 TIME STONED, DRAGGED OUT OF THE CITY, AND LEFT FOR DEAD**
Paul got up and walked back into the city. The next day he left.

 **MARTYRED**
In the end, he gave his life for his faith in Jesus Christ.

Despite it all, Paul said, **"I rejoice in what I am suffering for you."**
Colossians 1:24

A WORLD TRAVELER
PAUL SPREAD THE GOOD NEWS OF JESUS FAR AND WIDE.

ROME

PHILIPPI

THESSALONICA

GALATIA

COLOSSAE

TARSUS

EPHESUS

CORINTH

DAMASCUS

CAESAREA

JERUSALEM

- ● BIRTHPLACE
- † CONVERSION
- ⛪ CHURCHES PAUL WROTE TO
- 🏰 IMPRISONED

PAUL'S TRAVELS
COVERED MORE THAN
10,000 MILES.
THAT'S ABOUT THE DISTANCE FROM
LOS ANGELES,
CALIFORNIA TO
RIO GRANDE,
TIERRA DEL FUEGO

WALKING **5 MILES A DAY**
EVERY DAY,
THIS WOULD TAKE
5½ YEARS.

WALKING THIS DISTANCE
WOULD REQUIRE MORE THAN
20,000,000 STEPS.
THAT'S LIKE CLIMBING UP AND DOWN
THE EMPIRE STATE BUILDING
6,345 TIMES!

YOU'D PROBABLY BURN THROUGH
25 PAIRS OF SHOES
WALKING THAT MANY STEPS.

COUNTING ON GOD'S PROMISES FOR THE FUTURE

Exploring the Key Numbers in the Book of Revelation

7 IN THE BIBLE, THE NUMBER 7 REPRESENTS COMPLETION OR PERFECTION.

7

- **ANGELS** — REPRESENT
- **STARS**
- **CHURCHES** — SPEAK TO
- **LAMPSTANDS** — REPRESENT

Churches:
- EPHESUS
- SMYRNA
- PERGAMUM
- THYATIRA
- SARDIS
- PHILADELPHIA
- LAODICEA

HORNS on the Lamb

EYES on the Lamb

SEALS on the scroll of the Lamb

24 ELDERS bow to the Lamb

2 for each of the...

12 TRIBES of Israel

7 TRUMPETS blown by... **7 ANGELS** that bring... **7 JUDGMENTS**

7 BOWLS brought by... **7 ANGELS** that bring... **7 JUDGMENTS**

4 HORSES OF THE APOCALYPSE
- conquest
- war
- famine
- death

2 BEASTS oppose God and His people

1 DRAGON This fearsome creature is the devil himself, Satan.

144,000 people of Israel sealed for God

12,000 people from each tribe of Israel

1,000 years Christ reigns on earth and Satan is bound

0 TEMPLES God is dwelling with humanity

WITH WALLS 144 CUBITS THICK
30 AFRICAN ELEPHANTS could walk **side by side** on the top of the wall and have room to spare

144 cubits = **216 FEET**
12×12=144

12,000 STADIA

12,000 STADIA

1,380
1 stadia = 607 feet
12,000 stadia = 1,380 MILES wide, long, & high

A PERFECT CUBE just like the Most Holy Place in the tabernacle and temple, so big it would be about **HALF THE VOLUME OF THE MOON!**

THE NEW JERUSALEM

12,000 STADIA

THE NEW JERUSALEM IS 1,904,400 SQUARE MILES—ROUGHLY THE SIZE OF IRAN AND INDIA

636,313 SQUARE MILES

1,269,000 SQUARE MILES

COMBINED

These countries have a combined population of **1,414,280,000.**

12 PEARLS one on each gate, which is where we get the term "pearly gates."

12 ANGELS at the...

12 GATES bear the names of the...

12 TRIBES of Israel

12 FOUNDATION STONES bear the...

12 NAMES of the...

12 APOSTLES

12 JEWELS ADORNING THE FOUNDATION OF NEW JERUSALEM
The same ones found in the Garden of Eden and used as decorations in the tabernacle and temple.

 Jasper
 Sapphire
 Agate
 Emerald

 Onyx
 Carnelian
 Chrysolite
 Beryl

 Topaz
Chrysoprase
Jacinth
Amethyst

53

INDEX

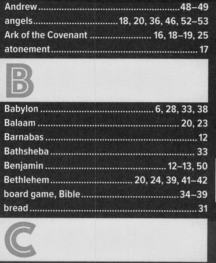

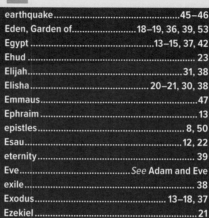

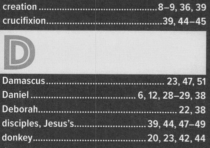

COMING SOON!

Learn more at **BibleInfographics.com**